MW00389756

A Musical for Senior Choir

Created and Arranged by Marty Parks

PUBLISHING COMPANY
KANSAS CITY, MO 64141

Contents

Joy to the World

ISAAC WATTS

GEORGE FREDERICK HANDEL
Arranged by Marty Parks

5

Joy to the world! the Lord is come; Let earth re-

ceive her King. Let ev-'ry heart pre-

pare Him room, And heav'n and na-ture sing, And Heav'n and na-ture

8

Memories of a Merry Christmas

DEBRA GRUBBS

MARTY PARKS
Arranged by Marty Parks

12

CD: 9 / 55

last thro'_ all our_ years.

32 Unison
Stee - ples chime and sleigh bells ring,

36
Voic - es join in car - ol - ing: "Si - lent Night" and

14

CD: 10 / 56

"We Three Kings"– all mem - 'ries of a mer-ry Christ - mas.

We're mak - ing mem - o - ries of a mer - ry Christ - mas in all we

see and do and hear; We're mak - ing mem - o - ries of a mer - ry

A Name I Highly Treasure

OSCAR C. ELIASON
and MARTY PARKS

OSCAR C. ELIASON
Arranged by Marty Parks

name ____ thro' which I find sal - va - tion. ____ No name on

earth ____ has meant so much to me. ____ I've learned to

love ____ the name an an - gel whis - pered So soft and sweet to Mar - y long a -

CD: 13 / 59

Solo
mp

mp

20

While Shepherds Watched Their Flocks

NAHUM TATE;
alt. Marty Parks

Traditional English Melody
Arranged by Marty Parks

CD: 16 / 62   Energetically ♩ = ca. 104

While shep-herds watched their flocks by night, All seat-ed

24

26

Away in a Manger

Anonymous

WILLIAM J. KIRKPATRICK
Arranged by Marty Parks

*Men sing cued notes only if necessary.

CD: 24 / 70

Caroling Medley
The First Noel
O Little Town of Bethlehem
We Wish You a Merry Christmas

Arranged by Marty Parks

*Parts optional throughout this medley

Born is the King_____ of Is - ra - el! No -

el,_____ No - el, No - el, No - el!

Born is the King_____ of Is - ra - el!

CD: 28 / 74

36

*"O Little Town of Bethlehem"

O lit - tle town of Beth - le - hem, How

still we see thee lie! A - bove thy deep and

dream - less sleep The si - lent stars go by. Yet

in thy dark streets shin - eth The ev - er - last - ing

38

39

40

wish you a mer-ry Christ - mas And a hap - py new year.

A

hap - py new

year!

Fairest Lord Jesus

Traditional German Hymn

Schlesische Volkslieder
Arranged by Marty Parks

CD: 33 / 79 Freely

In tempo ♩ = ca. 72

Men unison (Opt. choir unison)

Fair - est Lord Je - sus!

Rul - er of all na - ture! O Thou of

42

CD: 36 / 82

Son of _____ God and _____ Son of man! Glo - ry and hon - or, Praise, ad - o - ra - tion, Now and for - ev - er -

Go, Tell It on the Mountain

JOHN W. WORK, JR.

Afro-American Spiritual
Arranged by Marty Parks

CD: 38 / 84   Rhythmically

49

50

52

*Organ sustain chord to end

Memories of a Merry Christmas
[Reprise]

DEBRA GRUBBS

MARTY PARKS
Arranged by Marty Parks

We're mak-ing mem-o-ries of a mer-ry

Christ-mas in all we see and do and hear;

54

We're mak - ing mem - o - ries of a mer - ry Christ - mas that will

CD: 45 / 91

last thro'___ all our___ years. We're mak - ing

mem - o - ries of a mer - ry Christ - mas in all we see and___

years.   Mem - 'ries,

mem - 'ries   of a mer - ry

Christ - mas!

PRODUCTION IDEAS

Memories of a Merry Christmas is a musical designed for Senior Adult Choirs. Vocal ranges are kept within comfortable limits and the accompaniment is attainable by most pianists. The demonstration recording will offer some ideas on how the organ may be included as an additional accompanying instrument. The choir may be placed in the choir loft of your sanctuary or on risers, whatever best suits your purposes.

Props are to be simple and give a "living room" effect. A small table, maybe with a lamp on it, and a wing back chair or rocker are the main items. The narrator is a grandmother (a grandfather would work nicely as well) who throughout the musical is opening Christmas cards she's received and then shares thoughts and memories with the congregation. Be sure she has a strong speaking voice and is adequately miked. Memorization of lines would be an added bonus.

The grandmother enters about measure 41 of "Memories of a Merry Christmas," cards in hand (preferably already opened) and sits on the prop chair. Sipping a cup of coffee or hot tea would be a nice effect.

She should speak her lines with emotion, excitement or nostalgia depending on the particular passage. Consult the demonstration recording for presentation ideas. Find some Christmas cards that look similar to the ones she's describing so that she can look through them and perhaps hold them up for the congregation to see at the appropriate time.

Depending on your circumstances, the grandmother may or may not sing along with the choir during their numbers, but she should definitely sing along with the "Caroling Medley" and with the choir on "Memories of a Merry Christmas" reprise. If she's a soloist, consider having her sing the solo in "A Name I Highly Treasure."

The speakers for the "Remember When?" segment should use the printed material as a guide only. Encouraging your own choir and congregation to share their own funny or heart-touching Christmas memories would be much better. You may want to line up one or two "prompters" to get the ball rolling, but don't limit it to only three who offer anecdotes. Take your time through this section. By sharing at this time you're building some Christmas memories yourself!

You may reprint the lyrics for the "Caroling Medley" so that your congregation may sing along. No further permission is needed from the publisher.

SCRIPT

JOY TO THE WORLD

MEMORIES OF A MERRY CHRISTMAS

GRANDMOTHER: O hello there! I didn't see you come in, but I'm glad you're here. I don't get many visitors this time of year– everyone seems so busy. But I do get lots of cards. Why, just look at this stack…and this is only today's mail! I hope you don't mind if I take just a moment to look through these…it's the highlight of my day.

Seeing all the names on these cards sure brings back a lot of memories. Here's one from my brother, Stanley. Named for our father, you know; and he was named for his father. I suppose there are lots of dreams and aspirations that go along with maintaining a family name, and maybe just a touch of the right kind of pride. Names mean something, they say. It seems to me that that's why God chose a special name for His Son– a name given to Mary by an angel. A name that meant salvation.

O how I do love that name.

A NAME I HIGHLY TREASURE

GRANDMOTHER: Would you look at this? What a beautiful card! Shepherds on a hillside and the angel of the Lord above them in the sky. Now one thing bothers me, though. Why are the shepherds always pictured as men? Weren't there any lady shepherds? I guess that was in the days before equal employment opportunities!

Actually, I do remember a female shepherd…me, in the 5th grade and in our little church's Christmas pageant. There weren't many boys in our group and, well, we needed one more volunteer. That was me– "volunteered" by my mother. The most memorable part of the whole event was my one big speaking part. After the angel of the Lord announced the birth of Jesus, I was supposed to say, "Let us go now to Bethlehem and see this thing which has come to pass." Well, it didn't happen that way. I guess you could say I "froze." After stuttering and stammering for a few moments I finally blurted out, "We'd better scram!"

WHILE SHEPHERDS WATCHED THEIR FLOCKS

GRANDMOTHER: Hmm, here's a pretty card from my neighbor, Shirley. A holly wreath and an open Bible, surrounded by candles. I love candles and I just love going to our candlelight service at church on Christmas Eve. I've done it now for...well, a number of years. Something about the way the room glows when all those candles are lighted and we softly sing "Silent Night;" it always moved me as a child and, well, some things never change.

I used to imagine that we were all there at the stable in Bethlehem and the wooden manger scene at the front of the church was actually real. There among the animals were Joseph, Mary and the baby Jesus. I'd pretend that our small flames were the lanterns that illuminated the manger, giving warmth and light, allowing that sweet mother to see her precious Child as she sang Him His first lullaby.

AWAY IN A MANGER

GRANDMOTHER: Whenever my family gets together for Christmas, it's not long before we lapse into the "Remember when?" game. Some of the incidents we bring up seem to grow a little every year, and some get funnier each time they're told. I'm guessing it's the same with you and yours. So why don't we share a few Christmas memories right now?

(NOTE: the following are designed to be models. Encouraging the choir and congregation to share their own funny or heart-touching memories would be much, much better.)

SPEAKER 1: I remember one especially hectic Christmas season as I was raising my family. For some reason, the weeks before the big day had been nerve-wracking and then some. Unfortunately, Christmas Day didn't fare much better and the squabbling among the kids seemed to intensify as the day wore on. A few toys even got broken not long after they had been unwrapped.

Well, it came time for dinner and I asked our oldest son to return thanks. By that time about all he could mutter was a half-hearted rendition of the Lord's Prayer. That would have been all right, I suppose, except that about halfway through he groaned, "And forgive us our Christmases as we forgive those who Christmas against us."

SPEAKER 2: I'll tell you how times have really changed! Just last year I was at my daughter's house on Christmas Eve and as I stood admiring their lovely manger scene on the mantel, my little grandson, Joey, cozied up next to me. I lifted him in my arms and we began talking about the creatures and people we saw.

"Who's that?" I'd ask.
"Joseph," he'd answer.
"And who's that?"
"Mary."
"And that one?"
"Baby Jesus."
"And what's He lying in?"
"His car seat!"

SPEAKER 3: Well, my best Christmas memory isn't nearly so humorous as these, but it does bring me great joy. I remember the Christmas when, as a young man, the message of salvation through Jesus really hit home with me. When I finally realized that God became a man so that we could be forever with him, I just had to respond.

And so, one night, just a few days before Christmas, I knelt at my bedside and gave Him my heart. I don't really remember any of the gifts I received that year, but I do remember in vivid detail the change in my life and the deep peace I felt because I, too, had discovered the Christ of Christmas. I'll never forget the night and I'll never regret the choice.

GRANDMOTHER: Memories are a wonderful gift, aren't they? Even now when I hear the beautiful songs of Christmas, they remind me so much of my childhood and also the years of raising my own children and attending Christmas events together. But most of all, these songs remind me of God's unspeakable gift– His Son, Jesus.

And, you know, somehow when the carols begin, the words all seem to come back to me. It's just like when we used to go caroling in the neighborhood, trudging through the snow, laughing a lot and singing every Christmas song we could think of. We don't go caroling much anymore and I sure miss it.

But, wait! I think I hear some carolers right now! Why don't we join them?

CAROLING MEDLEY

GRANDMOTHER: O here's a card from my nephew, Andy. I must tell you what Andy did last year. It's something I know his family will remember and cherish all their lives. As he explains it, he simply got tired of decorating his Christmas tree with the same glass ornaments and twinkling lights he'd used for years. Still, he didn't know how to replace them. "These decorations, this entire season, it's all because of Jesus," he kept reminding himself.

Then it hit him. That little toy sheep from his son's miniature farm set would remind him of the "Lamb of God." And those alphabet blocks scattered all over the play room reminded him that Jesus is the "Word of the Father." Quickly he gathered up those along with dozens of other household items that reminded him of Christ and he decorated his tree in a new and most meaningful way.

He calls it his "Jesus Tree." After all, what's Christmas without Jesus? He honored us with His presence. Let's honor Him with our praise.

FAIREST LORD JESUS

GRANDMOTHER: Now, I just love this– a card from my granddaughter, Carrie. A few years ago she sent me a letter after Christmas listing in great detail every gift she'd received– color, size, how she'll use it…you get the point. I suppose it's natural. I did the same thing when I was young: telling everyone I saw about everything I'd received at every chance I got!

The way I see it, that's part of Christmas. The shepherds started it all, you know. They received word of a Savior, saw and experienced for themselves the new-born King, then told it to the whole countryside. "Spread abroad the news of this Child," the Bible says. God's wonderful gift of salvation for folks just like you and me. A lot of people need good news like that. The shepherds understood and they couldn't keep it to themselves.

Shouldn't we be doing the same thing?

GO, TELL IT ON THE MOUNTAIN

GRANDMOTHER: I'm so glad you stopped by for this visit. I've enjoyed it very much and I hope you'll come back. Maybe we could make it a tradition!

O before you leave, I have to share with you this one last card. The message isn't exactly what you'd expect, but I think it gives us wonderful guidelines for how to truly embrace the spirit of Christmas.

Here's what the card says:

THIS YEAR...
Mend a quarrel
Seek out a forgotten friend
Share a treasure
Give a soft answer
Encourage youth
Keep a promise
Forgive an enemy
Try to understand
Laugh a little
Laugh a little more
Express your gratitude
Speak your love
Speak it again
Speak it still again
Make a memory.

Merry Christmas, everyone!

MEMORIES OF A MERRY CHRISTMAS (Reprise)